EUROPA ⚔ MILITARIA
SPECIAL N⁰4

THE
ENGLISH CIVIL WAR
RECREATED IN
COLOUR PHOTOGRAPHS

CHRIS HONEYWELL
& GILL SPEAR

Windrow & Greene

Designed by John Anastasio/Creative Line

Printed in Singapore

This edition published
in Great Britain 1993 by
Windrow & Greene Ltd.
5 Gerrard Street
London W1V 7LJ

A CIP catalogue record for this book
is available from the British Library

ISBN 1-872004-54-7

Acknowledgements:
The authors and publisher wish to record their
gratitude for the generous assistance of many
people during the preparation of this
book, including particularly the following:
Nick Bacon, Mark Beaby, Peter Bentham Hill,
Gareth Blyth, John Crawford, Barry Denton,
Howard Giles, Mark Harrison, Chris Johnson,
Stuart Reid, Keith Roberts, David Ryan,
Margaret Smith, Kelvin Spooner, Des Thomas,
John Tincey, Dennis Ward, Tig Wright;
(at Basing House) Ian Barret, Simon Frame,
Phil French, Gerry Hughes, Geoff King,
Dave Laurent, John Litchfield, Andrew
Munro, Nigel Preece, Les Prince, Ian
Tindle, Alan Turton (Curator), Dave
Vogel, Ian Whittaker, David Wilson;
(at Clifford's Tower) Paul Cramer, Robert
Burrell Draper, Michael Fagin, Nigel Walton.
Particular thanks to all in Earl Rivers'
Regiment of Foot for their help over the years.

A Warre Without An Enemy

"Charge your pike..." The order from the grim-faced Royalist officer is almost drowned by an echoing volley of Parliamentarian musketry. Drums rattle out their urgent commands, and brightly coloured flags blow in the wind amidst the belching smoke of cannon-fire. A typical scene from the English Civil Wars: yet this is not 1642, but a Sunday afternoon three and a half centuries later. The Sealed Knot is once again in action.

Named after the Royalist underground organisation which plotted the restoration of the monarchy during Cromwell's Protectorate, today's **Sealed Knot Society** grew from a small private party held in 1967 to launch the book *Edgehill 1642: The Campaign and the Battle* by Brigadier Peter Young, a highly decorated wartime Commando officer and military historian. A very much larger than life character, Peter Young thought it might be fun if he and a few friends dressed up as Cavaliers; he could hardly have envisaged that the results would be so lasting or dramatic.

A few of Young's friends later wrote to ask when they could dress up again, and whether they could form a group to commemorate this formative period in our history. A man of action, Young saw the potential for something more adventurous than the original conception of a research and debating society. And so the Sealed Knot proper was born, at an inaugural meeting at The Mitre Hotel in Oxford; each of the founders undertook to recruit (sometimes reluctant) friends for a cross between a wargame and a military pageant.

From the beginning the society has owed one of its great strengths to Peter Young's insistence that membership be open to all who share its aims. The Knot has always been non-political, non-sectarian, and without bar on grounds of race, sex, age, or disability - each member contributes as much time and effort as he or she can manage. Some lady members "feign their sex" - which was not unknown in the 1640s - and march as soldiers; others encourage "living history" scenarios in camp and garrison displays. Every age from infants to grandparents can be seen at musters of the Knot.

Peter Young was the Sealed Knot's first, and hitherto only, Captain Generall - a position he held until his death in September 1988. The Knot owes much to the legacy of his charismatic personality; even in his last years he still rode his white charger around the battlefield to the applause of the crowd, and members still exchange affectionate anecdotes about this remarkable man.

The first musters were small in scope, and costume owed more to ingenuity than authenticity. Though a few members obtained Civil War-style helmets, the norm was bonded velvet uniforms, recycled "wellies", and plastic buff coats; tennis balls stood in for cannon-shot, pikes were extremely motley, and muskets were invariably shotguns with the addition of musket rests: as Peter Young said, "in those days we had 10% history and 90% imagination". Twenty-five years later the picture could not be more different; today's Sealed Knot members spend many hours researching every detail of Civil War clothing and armoury to achieve the most historically correct costumes possible. Muskets are authentic reproductions of 17th century matchlocks; 16-foot pikes are planed and balanced correctly to ease the proper exercise of this ancient weapon. The society is constantly striving to improve, and a whole sub-culture of small specialist businesses has sprung up to supply members' needs.

Cavalry and artillery play an active role in Sealed Knot re-enactments. Horses are specially trained to

participate in the thick of battle, their riders making dashing and colourful charges dressed in authentic buff coats, armour, "lobstertail" helmets and massive boots; practical research is even beginning to produce authentic 17th century saddles. Members of the Trayne of Artillery have pursued demanding research into the design and reconstruction of wooden gun carriages, and the intricacies of foundry-cast iron and brass gun barrels.While fulfilling the strictest legal and safety requirements, the society has acquired a range of pyrotechnical skills to add to the spectacle, from simple blank cannon-fire and ground charges to the burning of mock-up villages.

Wherever possible regiments wear the correct coloured coats, and are recruited in the areas where their namesakes first saw action. One of the oldest, for example, is the King's Lifeguard of Foot, who wear red, and recruit strongly in Oxford and Nottingham; while Lord Saye and Sele's "bluecoats" recruit in the Midlands and Kent. Large towns may support more than one local unit; in London one may find Royalist members of Prince Rupert's Foot living only streets away from Roundheads of Samuel Jones's Regiment.

Although the Knot was originally a Royalist group, it was obvious that not all members shared Peter Young's enthusiasm for King Charles; and a Roundhead army was developed by the historian Dr.John Adair. The relationship between the two elements echoes, nevertheless, the famous words of the 1643 correspondence between Sir Ralph Hopton and his old comrade and new opponent Sir William Waller: " a warre without an enemy". Nature being what it is, it is

4

normal to see members of each side drinking happily together only hours after facing each other in battle; and mixed marriages between latter-day Roundheads and Cavaliers are not unknown.

Many members were surprised at the early musters to see cars stop and crowds gather along hedgerows, occasionally causing major traffic congestion. With ever-growing numbers wishing either to join the Knot or merely to watch it in action, and with regiments springing up literally from Land's End to John O'Groats, it was clear by the end of the 1960s that it would have to evolve into the more professionally organised society of today. Nevertheless, professionalism in the society's administration and the quality of its displays has not altered the Knot's essential character: all members, from the chairman to the newest pikeman, remain volunteers.

As branches and regiments grew the Knot organised itself in regions, one of the earliest and still most active being the Army of the North. Through its efforts one of the first major battle re-enactments fought was Marston Moor (a battle which will be dramatically repeated during its 350th anniversary year in 1994). The Knot is also very active in Scotland, where the society takes on a new dimension from plaid-wearing Highlanders and dour, bonneted Covenanters. These Scots think nothing of travelling 500 miles during a weekend to take part in a battle in England, and hold their own musters at sites such as Stirling. The Knot is also developing

international links, with members in Germany and North America forming regiments and organising battles and "living history" camps; there have also been exchange visits between groups and individuals, and Sealed Knot displays in France and Germany.

As the society developed during the 1970s its numbers grew until Sealed Knot battles could involve a thousand participants; today three times that number may attend a major muster such as Newark or Edgehill in 1992, and with a paid-up membership of more than 6,000 the Knot is the largest active re-enactment association in Europe.

From its modest beginnings the society has also become a major charity fund-raiser - a role planned by Peter Young from the first. Apart from battles, Knot members and units also undertake many other sponsored events. The high identification with charity work has led great fortified houses such as Sudeley, Broughton Castle and Warwick Castle to invite the Knot on a regular basis to recreate past times, raising money for various causes. Councils and local charities such as the Lions and Rotary Clubs often join with the Knot in events such as the traditional Holly Holy Day at Nantwich, Cheshire, or major occasions such as those organised at Newark in Nottinghamshire. Wherever the Sealed Knot appears it draws substantial crowds, to the extent that its absence from a given event now causes comment.

In 1977 the Sealed Knot had the great honour of forming a guard of honour for H.M. The Queen at the Windsor firework display mounted as part of the Royal Silver Jubilee celebrations. Although it has always attracted press and television attention, the Knot has recently begun to receive approaches for film work as extras and specialists; having a ready-trained army of period soldiers enabled the society to fulfill military roles for such TV drama series as *By The Sword Divided* and *The Year of the French.*

Another important aspect of the activities of the re-enactment societies is historical research. From their roots in Peter Young's scholarship, the Knot and the ECWS have contributed greatly to serious enquiry into aspects of the period not suitable or fashionable for general academic study. Practical experiment and documentary research have combined to increase our understanding of subjects as varied as 17th century dyestuffs, and cooking, as well as clothing design and procurement, weapons and tactics. Valuable specialist publishing has been undertaken by society members; and professional historians such as Dr.David Chandler of the RMA Sandhurst, and the New Model Army authority Barry Denton, contribute their strength in research. The Knot is constantly asked for advice, at every level, on all aspects of the period.

The Sealed Knot is currently heavily involved in the celebrations for the 350th anniversary of the Civil Wars; and in 1993 enjoys its own Silver Jubilee, with justifiable pride in having not only fulfilled Peter Young's original intention of widening a nation's interest in its heritage, but also becoming a pleasurable part of everyday life for thousands of people.

In the early 1970s a second society was born out of the Sealed Knot. The **English Civil War Society** in fact consists of two virtually autonomous groups: **The King's Army** and **The Roundhead Association.** Contact between the Sealed Knot and the ECWS continues on an informal basis; there is considerable dual membership, and joint events are not unknown. The ECWS has a total membership of about 3,000, drawn from all over the country and with a small but stalwart contingent from the American colonies. The King's Army and Roundhead Association are each organised as a 17th century army, with a regiment of cavalry and several infantry regiments apiece, together with supporting artillery and camp-followers.

Though generally smaller than SK musters, ECWS displays have been notable recently for the society's 5

Association have combined at Warkworth Castle, Northumberland to recreate the Civil War garrison - Major William Lyell's company of the Master of Yester's Regiment.

The ECWS annual programme is carefully balanced to provide four evenly-spaced major events involving full musters of the membership, and anything up to 60 smaller "regimental invited events" of all shapes and sizes. These involve only a limited number of units as such, although members from other regiments can normally take part by joining the ranks of the invited units to ensure a convincing display.

The society has also been very active in promoting "living history" as distinct from purely military displays. In August 1986 the ECWS pioneered the use of English Heritage sites by re-enactment groups with a display at Tynemouth Castle; and since then has enjoyed a healthy relationship with English Heritage, presenting a number of impressions of garrison life each year.

Barry Denton FRHistS
Stuart Reid

ability to form and maintain recognisable battle-lines. The Roundhead Association, and less formally the King's Army, have formed brigades which group two or more units into larger formations. These are better suited to practising 17th century tactical evolutions without breaking down into formless, swirling mêlées.

Each ECWS unit is modelled on an original CivilWar regiment. All the recreated King's Army units served in, or alongside, the Royalist Oxford army in the summer of 1643. This allows a fairly tight specification for clothing and equipment, since the Oxford army was the best documented of all Royalist forces. The Roundhead Association covers a wider period, representing units from both the provincial armies of 1642-44 and the New Model Army and its successors, though "redcoats" predominate. Standards of costume authenticity are taken very seriously in both armies.

One Scottish-based RA unit, the Earl of Loudon's Regiment, in fact serves quite often on the Royalist side in post-1647 scenarios, given the complexity of Anglo-Scottish relations during the Civil Wars. Such flexibility is also seen in the occasional emergence of temporary units: e.g. the mainly English Royalist Sir Thomas Tyldesley's Regiment adopts the identity of the Laird of Grant's Regiment at Scottish events. Similarly, and particularly at events where the "living history" aspect is strong, a specific unit will be specially recreated to re-enact particular circumstances. On two occasions so far members of the King's Army and Roundhead

Pike

A pikeman of Devereux's Regiment of the English Civil War Society (hereafter, "ECWS") photographed at Basing House, the major Royalist stronghold in Hampshire which was the scene of much bloody fighting between July 1643 and October 1645. Apart from a steel gorget or collar-piece he wears the full recommended equipment of the pikeman. Helmets of various styles based on the older morion and cabasset were normal; this typical "pikeman's pot" has the morion's deep reinforcing comb and flared brim, and broad cheek-pieces. His waist-length back-and-breast plates are fitted with tassets - heavy thigh-pieces. He wears gloves to protect his hands when handling the pike; and has a simple, mass-produced sword ("a good stiff tuck") as a hand-to-hand weapon - in practice it was probably used for camp chores more often than for fighting. Early in the war many pikemen seem to have discarded first the tassets, and later the whole cuirass (which at up to 50lbs. weight was tiring to wear for any length of time); and many may never have received one in the first place. Armour was of limited practical use, seldom being proof against musket balls at battle ranges. On the march armour and sometimes pikes seem to have been carried in wagons (when available, and when battle was not imminent).

By the reign of King Charles I, England had enjoyed almost unbroken peace since the beginning of the 17th century; and, as a nation, had no continuity of military experience to draw upon when civil war broke out. Over the previous half-century, however, important advances had been made on the Continent in military equipment, training, formations and tactics. These had first emerged during the wars in Italy, and had developed further during the long struggle for Dutch independence from Spain, and latterly during Sweden's involvement in the Thirty Years' War. The campaigns of Maurice of Nassau and Gustavus Adolphus had been the talk of Europe. Thousands of British mercenaries had served overseas, and in the 1640s many brought their first-hand experience home. Professional soldiers and drill-masters had published technical treatises in English, which were studied by the keener officers of the Trained Bands regional militia.

In the early campaigns of the Civil War the leaders struggled to impose these professional models on the raw mass of indifferently equipped, poorly disciplined, and unreliably paid volunteer and conscript recruits. But bloody experience provided its own instruction: and by the 1650s British regiments seem to have been the professional equals of any in Europe.

*   *   *

The Civil War "regiment of foot" was organised on a theoretical model of ten companies totalling either 1,000 or 1,200 men plus officers. In practice the regiments' uneven success in recruiting, variable rate of desertions, and good or bad fortune in disease-ridden camps and on the battlefield left them with anything between 150 and 850 men, with some extreme examples even weaker or stronger; and the number of companies raised could also vary.

Despite the growing dominance of musketeers on the mid-17th century battlefield their vulnerability to cavalry during the reloading process still made it necessary to mix them for protection with blocks of pikemen. The proportion of "shot" to "pike" varied, generally increasing steadily from about two-to-one in 1642; many units, particularly Royalist, were all-shot by 1645. Each company had a mixed strength;

the pike was supposedly the more honourable weapon, and for practical reasons was carried by the strongest men.

On the battlefield the company did not fight as a tactical formation; a strong regiment might be divided into two "grand divisions", while weaker regiments might form a single unit, or in extreme cases several regiments might be combined. Within the tactical units (called "battalia") all the pikemen were drawn up in a central block between two wings of musketeers, all formed six or eight men deep. The basic sub-unit was the file - that is, the six or eight men who stood in a line from front to rear of the formation. In theory there were set positions for men of different experience and seniority within each file, the senior man taking the lead.

(**Below**) A sergeant of John Bright's Regiment, ECWS, photographed at Clifford's Tower in York - an artillery position during the siege of 1644. He represents a member of Sir Thomas Fairfax's Parliamentarian army in the north of England, identified by the blue sash; the flat woollen bonnet and plain grey coat were typical of both Scots Covenanters and northern English troops. Body armour would not have been general in the northern army, which had much more "shot" than "pike"; but like the sash, and the modest lace decoration on the breeches, it is a typical distinction for a junior officer (among whom sergeants were then classed). Sergeants were officially distinguished by carrying halberds - axe-headed polearms. He wears a typical sleeveless buff coat with shoulder extensions; and ankle-length "start-ups", old-fashioned but hard-wearing labourers' boots.

(**Above**) A lieutenant of Devereux's Regiment, ECWS, at Basing House. In theory each company had a captain, a lieutenant, and an ensign. Officers wore their own personal clothing, displaying a greater or lesser degree of wealth. This young gentleman has fine lace shirt cuffs and collar ("falling band"), its points gathered by a ribbon; a hat with expensive imported plumes; gold bullion lace on his breeches; and fashionably red-heeled "bucket top" riding boots, the tops folded down here for service on foot. In battle he might wear back-and-breast armour over his buff coat. Marks of officer rank are his gorget; his bullion-fringed sash, in the tawny-orange which identified the Earl of Essex's Parliamentarian army; and the partizan, a short polearm with a more or less elaborately shaped head - the tassel collar was practical as well as decorative, keeping rain from running down onto the grip. His sword is a reproduction of the so-called "mortuary" style: the crude human head worked into the basket guard has been claimed to commemorate the fate of King Charles the Martyr - but examples are known with female heads, and others which pre-date 1649.

(**Right**) Another pikeman of Devereux's Regiment, ECWS; and a close-up of his cuirass. Most Civil War armour was blackened or browned to protect it against rust, which on a wet day can bloom over polished steel surfaces almost while you watch.

Most helmets were apparently unlined, and worn over a knitted "Monmouth cap" - a very widespread piece of common soldier's headgear. For most Civil War soldiers the only item of actual "uniform", issued in a common colour to the men of a unit, was normally the coat; even this was far from universal - and a regiment might change its coat colour with each replacement issue. Otherwise soldiers were largely dressed in what they brought from their homes or managed to buy, steal or scavenge on campaign, with occasional issues of replacement shoes and shirts obtained by their quartermasters by the same methods but on a grander scale.

A re-enactor might spend today around £65 for a metal helmet, £95 for breast-and-back armour with tassets, £35 for his coat, £15 for his woollen breeches, £70 for a good pair of hobnailed reproduction 17th century "latchet" shoes, and anything between £65 and £95 for a sword, scabbard and baldric. With linen shirts, stockings, and small personal kit, a complete outfit costs £500 or £600; but most units have regimental stocks, and a recruit is not expected to buy the whole kit for his first muster.

(Above, left to right:) Pikemen photographed at a muster of the Sealed Knot (hereafter, "SK") at Carew Castle; the Marquis of Newcastle's Whitecoats at Edgehill; Earl Rivers' Regiment, Western Association at Weston Super Mare; and an officer of the King's Lifeguard at Edgehill. The latter wears a "Montero", a type of cap which seems to have been popular (particularly in the "Oxford army") throughout the Civil War.

(Left) Pikes, helmets, an officer's partizan and a sergeant's halberd laid ready for an SK muster at Roundway Down by Stamford's Regiment. Civil War ash-wood pikes varied from 15ft. to 18ft. but 16ft. was conventional, sometimes with wound twine

grips. Some soldiers disobediently cut theirs down to handier lengths; if battle brought them to "push of pike" against opponents with longer staves they might pay a grisly price. About two feet of the shaft below the 8in. head was usually protected against sword-cuts by riveted steel strips.

(Right) Second Battle of Newbury, SK: pikemen of Robert Hammond's Regiment on the march, pikes shouldered, with slung blankets and knapsacks. The Sealed Knot usually organise one long endurance march each year, in full kit and complete with wagons, following the historical route of a particular Civil War campaign. Such marches are sponsored for charitable causes.

(Above) Pikemen of the King's Lifeguard of Foot, SK, take up their positions at Weston Super Mare, holding their pikes at the "advance". The English "lobster-tail pot" helmet with its three-bar face guard was primarily a cavalry item, but would have been worn by some officers of foot. The original Lifeguard were not a picked elite, but an ordinary regiment - often understrength and badly armed, like other early Royalist units - raised in Derbyshire, Lincolnshire and Cheshire. They were, however, issued with uniforms: complete red suits and Monteros.

The difficulty of handling the 16ft. pike in closely-ordered ranks without tripping or even maiming ones comrades must have made recruit drill parades a sight to behold. Officers would have been satisfied when their men could handle the unwieldy weapon deftly enough to form up and march without disruption or injury; and to present an effective, overlapping hedge of points for attack and defence.

(Right) A plain, soldierly-looking officer at Carew Castle; in the background, pike of the Lifeguard and Rivers' Regiment, SK. His gorget, sash and partizan mark his status; and note the fashionable open, buttoned coat sleeves. The staves of some halberds and partizans were covered with leather or fabric, and/or studded with brass (which does not rust or spark, and wears down smoothly without snagging); for cheapness and safety re-enactors often use painted wooden heads for combat. Officers work their way up through the ranks of their re-enactment units; they are trained in the use of all arms, and have to pass safety tests on their handling before promotion to posts of responsibility.

(Below) Second Battle of Newbury, SK: pikemen of Slanning's Regiment and (background) the Western Association move into the attack. Striped pike staves are used by this re-enactment unit for identification. Some re-enactors use headless staves, others heads of carved and painted wood or of vulcanised rubber, for cheapness and safety (metal heads are expensive and easily damaged).

(**Below**) Second Battle of Newbury, SK: an artillery gun captain – note his linstock, and the whip for gun team horses – warns a sergeant of Western Association pikemen: "Have a care, loaded gun!" A Civil War company was supposed to have two sergeants and three corporals for 100 or so privates (the term was already in use); but in the early campaigns there was a chronic shortage of experienced sergeants.

Weston Super Mare and Second Battle of Newbury, SK: pike press, "Bertie Basset's Regiment" - the name given to temporary units formed at musters by amalgamating smaller groups into a regiment of practical size for battle. The rear ranks of Civil War pike units would have packed in behind their front-rank comrades with staves slanted, shoving on their backs to lend weight and momentum. Very much the same happens in re-enactments, most pike units fighting with points upward for the sake of safety; for the same reason swords are not carried by pikemen in battle. Such encounters have been described as like "rugby matches with 600 a side".

Shot

The smoothbore, muzzle-loading, matchlock muskets used in the Civil War - like so much other equipment, in a country pitched into war without the well-stocked magazines of a standing army - came from various British and foreign sources, and were of various ages, lengths and bores. Before the war the usual barrel length was about 4ft., the bore being calculated on a bullet size of 12 to the pound weight (roughly .8 inch). With a weight of 14 to 20lbs. this heavy musket required a forked rest for efficient aiming, adding to the burden and awkwardness of the musketeer's equipment. A "bastard musket" with a 3ft.6in. barrel was also available; at 10 to 12lbs. this could be aimed without a rest, but supplies of all kinds were uncertain, and mixed equipment within armies and regiments was common.

Differing bores caused problems of ammunition supply, and soldiers had to clip or even bite bits of lead off the issued bullets to make them fit the barrel. Gunpowder was supposed to be issued in two grades of fineness: "corn" powder for the main charge, and a finer grain "touch" powder for priming the small external pan, which flared when set off by the smouldering match. Powder quality was sometimes as unpredictable as ball size; and by some accounts Civil War musketeers were careless about carrying paper for wadding, even further reducing accuracy and rate of fire.

The bandolier of wooden or tin tubes in which the musketeer carried 12 to 16 measured charges of powder (not, in fact, called "the Twelve Apostles" in the 17th century) was certainly awkward to use. The tube covers could slip up their strings, spilling powder; in battle a man could easily forget which ones he had emptied; they rattled loudly, betraying night attacks and ambushes; and with burning matchcords and opened powder containers all round him in a close engagement, it was not unknown for a soldier to suffer the lethal explosion of his whole bandolier.

An alternative was some sort of belt-box worn at the waist, holding measured charges in folded paper cartridges; and these were issued to some extent. But paper cartridges often came apart with hasty handling or simply from being shaken up on the move. Some commanders complained of men carrying cartridges in their pockets, where they quickly spoiled; and even of some "fantastical fellows" loading by eye from handfuls of loose powder. At least paper cartridges provided their own wads.

In the days of flint-and-steel and tinderbox the need to keep matchcord smouldering whenever battle was imminent was a problem, and soldiers must constantly have been asking a comrade or their file-leader for a light. Once lighted, they normally kept both ends smouldering at once in case one end got extinguished or was blown off by the detonation of the priming. An

(continued on page 21)

Musketeer, Colonel Valentine Walton's Regiment, ECWS, photographed at Basing House. Civil War musketeers did not wear helmets, or any other armour. The broad-brimmed felt hat was a desirable, though quite expensive headgear in mid-17th century armies; this soldier has a piece of paper tucked into the cord as a "field sign". Since units on opposing sides often wore the same coloured coats, or no uniform clothing at all, cases of mistaken identity were frequent, often leading to death or capture. Officers were identifiable only by coloured sashes, of which the best-known are Essex's Parliamentary tawny-orange and the King's red. Before an engagement field signs such as sprigs of greenery, pieces of paper, scraps of cloth or even untucked shirt tails were often chosen, as were battle-cries and passwords.

Many soldiers were issued with a "snapsack" to carry a few spare clothes, rations, utensils, and small belongings such as flint-and-steel. This sturdy leather example is of a less popular shape; most were sausage-shaped, of thin leather or light canvas. This soldier also has a fine glazed stoneware bottle for his water (perhaps mixed with vinegar) or ale, in the Dutch style known as "bellarmine".

He wears simple over-stockings to protect the inner pair; the use of layered stockings and shirts seems to have been common. His plain, broad-bladed sword is worn from a baldric. Note the long ramrod ("scouring stick"), tipped with bone or copper to prevent sparking, in its housing under the barrel of his musket. The musketeer was supposed to carry detachable tools which screwed to the other end of this: a wire brush for scouring out a fouled barrel, and a corkscrew-shaped "worm" for drawing out misfires.

The musketeer of Walton's, showing his equipment. At least one powder flask, with a spring cut-off device in the nozzle to control the flow, would have been carried for the fine "touch" powder; and perhaps a second with a reserve of "corn" powder. On the hip a pouch for musket balls is just visible above the flask. He might also carry a small oil bottle; and, unless he was a fool,"proyning wires" to prick away the heavy fouling of burnt powder which after repeated firing could block the touch-hole connecting the priming pan and the charge in the barrel.

A supply of match, cut to convenient lengths, is looped to his belt of charges, and more may be tucked into his shirt or under his hat. Match was simply made by soaking cord in a saltpetre solution, which makes it smoulder slowly and evenly; on one famous occasion the Royalist general Sir Ralph Hopton supplied his troops by requisitioning bedstead cords from the householders of Devizes.

The wooden bottles for the powder charges were turned, proofed by soaking in oil, then painted or varnished. Re-enactors' charge bottles, though still made from wood, often have non-sparking copper lining for safety; and powder flasks are non-ferrous, spark proof, and have built-in weak spots. The issue of powder during re-enactments is tightly controlled, and unused powder must be handed back.

Would-be re-enactor musketeers must hold a Shotgun Certificate and a Black Powder Permit. They also have to attend four battles with dummy or unloaded muskets, to become accustomed to the adrenalin-rush which can occur during combat re-enactments. They are then tested on firing practice, maintenance and safety before obtaining a Proficiency Test card. All training is done through the regiment, but tests are by the Musket Inspectorate of the Safety Board, one of whose inspectors is present at every muster. Proficiency Test cards are revoked on the spot if anyone is seen using a musket unsafely.

(**Right**) Musketeer, Devereux's Regiment, ECWS, demonstrating the use of the musket rest, in the drill posture "Guard your pan". Note the thong round his left wrist, allowing him to let the rest drag when he needs both hands for reloading. Reproduction matchlock muskets are made by about half-a-dozen active gunsmiths in Britain; re-enactors may also buy them from their units. Most cost from around £110 upward. They weigh around 12lbs.; the bore is .75 to .88 in.; the steel barrels are fully proofed for shot, and numbered for tracing, to conform with legal requirements.

The knitted Monmouth cap was produced in tens of thousands by many contractors, apart from individually home-knit ones, and varied from a skimpy stocking cap to a large, felted, blocked item like this, using a pound weight of wool.

His coat is "uniform" in the sense that his commanders have ordered it in bulk in a common colour and lining; it may distinguish a regiment, or a larger regional force. It was not until 1646, when hostilities were almost over, that Parliament's New Model Army were able to issue a single colour throughout - red - with different coloured linings probably for different regiments (the lining presumably visible at turned-back cuffs). The coat was a heavy outdoor garment of dense broadcloth.

Under it the soldier wore his civilian clothes, supplemented by occasional army issues; these were for use, not identification, and although e.g. breeches seem often to have been grey, colours would be governed by cost and availability. A wool or heavy linen doublet, sometimes attached to the breeches, was often worn. Loose, lined broadcloth breeches were about calf-length (31in. is a measure mentioned in accounts lists), gathered by garters; leather pockets were common. Loose linen shirts had small collars and gathered cuffs; more than one might be worn in cold weather. Long knit or woven stockings were normally grey or white. Civil War armies knew the importance of good footwear, and tried (ideally) to replace the sturdy, straight-lasted, round- or square-toed "latchet" shoes about every three months.

(**Right**) Reliance on a burning match could leave units of "shot" helpless at short notice in rainy weather (even very damp air increases the rate of misfires to anything up to 50 per cent). Naked flame and loose powder was a recipe for frequent accidents. Night attacks were often betrayed by the tell-tale points of light. Free from all these drawbacks were the early flintlock ("firelock") muskets, available to Civil War armies in small numbers. Needing no naked flame, they could be carried loaded but uncocked for hours, ready for instant use. Costing half as much again as a matchlock (in 1645, 15s.6d. - three weeks' pay for a soldier), they were normally carried only by special picked infantry units; and particularly by musketeers guarding the artillery, where smouldering match close to open powder barrels could cause catastrophic accidents. This musketeer of Walton's Regiment has a "dog-lock" flintlock, named from the safety catch visible behind the cock.

(**Left**) An officer of Devereux's Regiment of the Roundhead Association, ECWS. This might be described as "daily" military dress; back-and-breast plates might be added for battle. The felt hat was quite a costly item in the 17th century, as were imported feather plumes - de rigeur for a fashionable officer. The opening, buttoned doublet sleeves are typically banded with gold bullion lace; he has a fine lace collar falling over his gorget, and extra "boot hose" protect expensive stockings from the rubbing of his superb bucket-top boots, fitted with spurs on "butterfly" leathers for riding - an infantry officer would ride on the march. The broad fringed sash, tied in a huge bow, is typical. A more decorative and less functional "leading staff" might be carried instead of a partizan.

A regiment of foot might have a staff of a colonel, a lieutenant-colonel, a sergeant-major (then an officer rank), a quartermaster, a provost-marshal; and perhaps 27 other company officers. Both sides, but particularly the Royalists, suffered as the war progressed from an excess of officers. Regimental strengths were whittled away by disease, death and desertion; but reduced units only grudgingly amalgamated with others, the officers refusing to give up their status and pay. (The Royalist garrison of Reading in 1644 included Blackwell's Regiment, of four companies, with a total of 56 men but 30 officers.) In both armies, but particularly the King's, officers without soldiers might fight in the ranks, sometimes forming whole troops or companies. These "reformadoes" did not enjoy a high reputation for discipline or efficiency.

army on campaign used vast quantities of matchcord, and ensuring supplies was a major logistic problem: one threatened garrison of 1,500 men is recorded as having used some quarter-ton weight of match in 24 hours.

Parliament's armies at first favoured an eight-rank formation for the wings of musketeers flanking the "stands" of pike when drawn up for battle, but the Royalists may have adopted the Swedish six-rank style by the battle of Edgehill; by 1643 this seems to have been the norm on both sides. As the battle lines approached one another musketry was used to thin and disrupt the enemy's ranks. Although a musket ball could kill at 600 yards, and pierce armour at 200-400, it was hopelessly inaccurate at such distances. Individual marksmanship was generally unknown in pitched battles; the unit of shot fired "into the brown", by ranks, on their officer's order. Unless trying to provoke the enemy for some reason they seldom opened fire at more than 100 yards' range. Even then the effect was uncertain; but a solid hit, by luck or judgement, with a large, slow, soft-lead ball caused lethally mangling wounds.

The classic Dutch system used by both sides involved each rank of musketeers firing in turn, then retiring to the rear to reload. Variations of this system could be carried out while maintaining the same ground or while advancing or retreating; the object was to keep up a continuous fire (experiments prove that a competent musketeer could reload in about half a minute).

(Below) English Civil War Society musketeers assemble in York, March 1993, to take part in a march and wreath-laying ceremony to honour the memory of the great Civil War general and gentleman Sir Thomas Fairfax, creator and leader of Parliament's New Model Army. The scarlet-uniformed men of Devereux's Regiment in the foreground wear Montero caps; the upper flaps could sometimes be folded in various ways to give protection from the weather - before the Civil War the Montero was already known in Germany as the "English fog-hat". Note also bandoliers of charges with blue-painted tubes and blue-and-white strings; these colours are specified in the surviving contract books of the New Model Army.

(Left) Musketeers of the King's Lifeguard, SK, at Carew Castle, carrying rests and reversed muskets; at left is a sergeant.

(Below left & right) Ranks of SK northern Parliamentarians, including Ballard's Greycoats, fire a "salvee" at Edgehill. This Swedish variation on the usual rolling fire by ranks was well established in Continental wars before the 1640s. In the last moments before two bodies of foot came together, the ranks of "shot" might be doubled up to fire three ranks together - the front rank kneeling, the next stooping and the third standing behind them. By doubling their frontage all six ranks might even fire at once. This concentrated firepower might decimate the enemy front ranks at the psychological moment before hand-to-hand contact, but left musketeers with no time to reload.

(**Right**) Royalist musketeers of Sir Marmaduke Rawdon's Regiment, SK, fire a volley during a muster at Weston Super Mare, the barrels pointing up for safety.

These photographs show "shot" of the Tower Hamlets Trained Bands, SK, during a muster at Weston Super Mare. The Trained Bands were local militias first raised in Queen Elizabeth's reign, which by 1642 varied widely in strength, equipment and preparedness; but they were the nearest thing England had to a standing army, and both sides tried to get control of them (and their armouries) by selective appointment of officers. Most Trained Bands refused to serve outside their counties. Notable exceptions were those from Cornwall, who were among the King's best infantry; and the London Trained Bands, who were from the first among Parliament's most valuable assets. The Bands of the city and suburbs totalled, by 1643, nine very strong regiments (averaging about 1,200 men each) and nine new Auxiliary regiments of 1,000 each. A reliable Parliamentary defence force for the capital, the London Trained Bands were also persuaded to supply large field brigades for campaigns further afield in 1643-44.

(Left) Note the pronounced "hatchet" shape of the musket stock; the cloth field sign tied around a sleeve, left; and this re-enactor's basket-hilted sword, rather more elaborate than would normally be seen at the hip of a simple soldier.

(**Left and below**) Under the orders of a sergeant at the far end of the ranks, the Tower Hamlets men (to judge from their colours in the background, from the second captain's company - see page 32) make ready to fire. As with the pike, technical treatises included dozens of drill postures each with its own word of command, giving an impression of complexity. In wartime practice the handling of the weapon would be learned as a logical sequence and the number of separate commands would be reduced to the minimum necessary for safety and the effective delivery of fire in battle: ambitious enough objectives, when working with recruits many of whom would never have held a gun in their lives.

(**Left**) Tower Hamlets shot drawn up in two ranks; the mix of muskets used with and without rests is probably authentic. Before re-enactors who use rests close with the enemy in hand-to-hand combat they drop their rests - the spiked ferrule could be dangerous; they also discard any pieces of lighted match for the same reason - young "powder monkeys" follow up the regiment to collect them. Note large brass and small leather-covered powder flasks, and spare matches.

The essential stages of reloading a matchlock musket; these actions must be repeated before each shot.

(Left) A green-coated musketeer of Carr's Regiment, SK, at Carew Castle. He has removed the smouldering match from the spring jaws of the "serpent" and holds it safely out of the way between the fingers of his left hand. With his right he selects and opens a charge bottle, and prepares to pour powder into the muzzle.

(Right) Men of Bright's and Hampden's Regiments, Crawford's Brigade, ECWS, at Gosport. The ball was then dropped into the muzzle after the powder, with or without a paper wad; these men now ram home their (blank) charges. In the excitement and confusion of battle it is surprisingly easy to fire a musket with the ramrod still in the barrel, with dangerous consequences. The explicit order to "secure your scouring stick" is always given before the order to fire, and musketeers learn the habit of feeling for it under the barrel.

(Below left) A musketeer of Devereux's, ECWS, at Basing House. The swivelling cover is now swung off the priming pan; "touch" powder is poured in; and the pan is re-covered.

(Below centre) After any spilt priming powder is carefully blown off the outside of the lock the match is replaced in the serpent.

(Below right) The musketeer has to adjust the length of his match every few moments as it burns away, or the smouldering tip will no longer fall squarely on the powder in the priming pan when he finally pulls the trigger. He also has to blow on the match to remove the fine ash and keep the tip glowing hot.

(**Right**) "Give fire!" - Goring's Regiment, King's Army, ECWS, at the Gosport muster. When the trigger was pulled the serpent snapped down and back, pressing the glowing tip of the match into the priming powder. A simpler way, sometimes used *in extremis,* was to ignore the serpent and simply to hold a length of match in the right hand, "popping" it directly into the priming at the order to fire; the reduction in accuracy was not too important at very close ranges. Either way, the "hang-fire" before the priming sets off the main charge in the barrel can seem surprisingly long.

(**Above**) The tension of waiting: a Sealed Knot musketeer awaits the enemy during a muster at Northampton.

(**Right**) Men of a mixed ECWS formation stand steady in their ranks, the front rank in the "present" position, with priming pans uncovered, straining for the order to fire. Since he has no match the foreground man seems to be a trainee musketeer serving out his safety apprenticeship with an unloaded musket.

Colours and Drums

Each company of a Civil War infantry regiment had its own flag - the "colour" or "ensign". Surviving evidence shows that while those of the various regiments differed quite widely, there was a common system of design. A typical (though far from universal) scheme was as follows:

The senior "colonel's company" colour might be a plain field in a colour common to all the regiment's ensigns. The "lieutenant colonel's" was plain apart from a St.George's Cross in the upper hoist corner. The "sergeant-major's company" often had the same but with a wavy "pile" in a contrasting colour diagonally from the bottom right corner of the St.George's Cross. The ensigns of the "captains' companies" bore the St.George's Cross, plus from one to seven symbols - discs, diamonds, crosses, stars, etc. - in the contrasting colour, arranged in lines or block patterns, the number of symbols identifying the company. Different conventions adopted for the ensigns of the senior officers' companies make it difficult to identify any particular captain's colour with certainty unless the whole regimental scheme is known.

(Above) Battle of Roundway Down, SK: colours and drums of the Parliamentary force assembled during a parley.

(Left) Royalist ensigns at the battle of Edgehill, SK: right, that of a company of Charles Gerard's Regiment - one of several units with quartered colours and unusual company distinctions.

30

(**Left**) Weston Super Mare, SK: second captain's colour, Sir Thomas Ballard's Regiment. Civil War colours were about 6ft.6in. square, of painted silk, flown on quite short staves which allowed the bearers to perform elaborate ceremonial flourishes. For economy, today's reproductions are sometimes made of linen or cotton, and cost around £25 - silk reproductions can cost around £100, and colours are easily damaged in battle. The colour was carried by the junior company officer,the term "ensign" also being used for this rank.

(**Right**) A Parliamentary officer photographed at Basing House carrying the 1649 Commonwealth Ensign adopted after the First Civil War and the King's execution. Over his blue doublet he wears a gorget, a baldric for his swept-hilt rapier, and a tawny-orange sash. His outer garment is a "cassack", with unbuttoning sleeves and side seams which allowed it to be arranged either as a coat or a cloak. Cheaper alternatives were simple cloaks of various lengths, often worn by cavalry; and the "Dutch coat", a conventional loose overcoat.

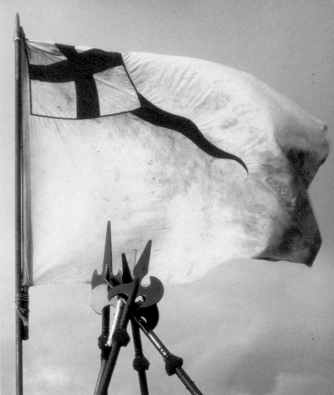

(**Left**) The colours of the Tower Hamlets Trained Bands regiment of Parliamentary foot were clearly recorded, and one is carried here by Sealed Knot re-enactors at Weston Super Mare. The whole regiment carried red colours with the silver central motto JEHOVA PROVIDEBIT ("God Will Provide") surrounded by palm branches, with small palms in the corners, all except the colonel's having the St.George's Cross in the upper hoist canton. The sergeant-major's bore a single disc at the top edge beside the cross, instead of the alternative "pile"; so the first captain's bore two discs, the second captain's three (as here, with one disc obscured), and so on.

(Far left) Roundway Down, SK: blue ensign of a regiment using a motif from its commander's heraldic arms instead of simple geometric shapes. (Left) Weston Super Mare, SK: white ensign with "pile" identifying the sergeant-major's company. (Right) Pendennis Castle, SK: a white-on-black colonel's company colour, carried by the recreated Sir Nicholas Slanning's Regiment.

(Left) Second Battle of Newbury, SK: ensigns of Prince Rupert's Regiment of Foot had a black and white quartered design with companies identified by numbers of open circles. At least four were captured at Naseby in 1645 (where, with some 500 men, it may have been the strongest Royalist unit of foot on the field), and were later recorded when paraded in London. Female regimental musicians, with a fife and a small side drum, are seen in the background wearing laced coats with open sleeves; boy and girl members of re-enactment units often take the field in this guise.

(**Left**) Sealed Knot drummer boy of the King's Lifeguard of Foot in camp at Roundway Down. Each infantry company officially had two drummers; when the unit was drawn up for battle they, like their officers and sergeants, took post on the flanks of the blocks of pike and shot where they could - in theory - be seen and heard. Civil War drummers were not in fact boys; the drums were large and heavy, and drummers had a vital part to play in battle, beating signals to pass their officers' orders. They also still retained echoes of the medieval herald, being sent as envoys to parley with the enemy (and, if possible, to spy out his forces). These duties demanded maturity and intelligence.

(**Right**) Drummer, Colonel Valentine Walton's Regiment, ECWS, photographed at Basing House. Drummers' clothing was not regulated, but as they played an important part in the regiment's outward show the colonel normally paid for a more or less elaborate costume. One very common feature was the coat with opened, hanging sleeves. A sword was worn as a sign of military dignity rather than a practical weapon. This rope-tensioned field drum is of authentic size and weight, made of Dutch oak, goatskin and calfskin. It is carried by means of the silk sash - which can cut off the circulation after three hours' unrelieved carrying of the drum. Reproduction drums are purchased by regiments from specialist makers, and cost from about £130.

Horse

In theory a Civil War cavalry regiment was about 500 strong, divided into six troops. In practice it might have anything from 150 to (exceptionally) 800 or more men, in from three to ten troops. A troop conventionally had one captain, one lieutenant, one cornet, a quartermaster, three corporals, two trumpeters, a farrier, and anything from 25 to 80 troopers.

Early in the war the Royalists, recruiting among the rural gentry and their followers, enjoyed advantages both in numbers and in quality of cavalry to offset Parliament's advantages in mercantile wealth and urban militia infantry. Prince Rupert of the Rhine, the King's nephew, was a brilliant and experienced cavalry general; his example dominated cavalry tactics for much of the war. By 1645, however, Parliament had patiently redressed the balance. The New Model Army cavalry - particularly the units formed from Oliver Cromwell's old Eastern Association regiments - were equal in all respects, and superior in discipline, to the Cavalier horse.

Although many cavalry units spent much of the war split up for dispersed garrison duties, their tactics when assembled for pitched battle were fairly predictable. The cavalry of the

Second Battle of Newbury: a veteran owner-rider trooper of Sir William Waller's Lifeguard, SK, presents the classic outline of a Civil War "harquebusier". It is difficult to obtain convincing-looking 17th century-style tack,

although there is a saddler in Fareham, Hampshire, who makes reproduction bridles, and there is a move towards a standard bridle. Since horses cannot easily adjust to different bits these will remain modern.

opposing armies were almost invariably drawn up in one or two lines on each wing, flanking the massed infantry centre. At some point they would fight each other, the winners then being free to return and take the enemy infantry in the rear and flanks. The normal cavalry unit formation was in three ranks, with one horse-length space between ranks, although Parliamentary cavalry at first tried a Dutch six-rank system.

Like the great Gustavus Adolphus of Sweden, Prince Rupert favoured shock tactics - the thundering charge, sword in hand. Only when his troopers were in amongst the now-disordered enemy were they to use their pistols and carbines at point-blank range.

Parliament's leaders at first attempted a more deliberate Dutch style, sending their horsemen forward one rank at a time to fire into the enemy, weakening them for a final

Waller's trooper exercising on the morning before Second Newbury. He has a rolled blanket, cloak and fodder sack behind his saddle; a pair of pistols, with flask and pouch, in saddle holsters; and a slung flintlock carbine, copied from surviving examples in the Littlecote House collection.

Early in the Civil War most horses, certainly in the Royalist armies, would have been provided by their riders or unit commanders. The task of keeping armies mounted as the war progressed was enormous, and every means was used: central purchase, hire-purchase, compulsory regional quotas, quasi-legal confiscation, and outright theft. The cost of a cavalry horse varied between about £6 and £10 (for comparison: 10-16 days' pay for a captain, six to 10 months' pay for a soldier).

sword-charge. If charged themselves the troopers were supposed to hold their ground until the last moment before firing into the approaching enemy, then drawing sword to meet them hand-to-hand.

Royalist commanders seldom gave their opponents time for such complicated tactics; the unevenly trained Roundhead troopers could seldom stand their ground in the face of a Cavalier charge, and Rupert's regiments swept them from the field time after time.

By 1645, however, Parliamentarian units such as Cromwell's famous "Ironsides" had been patiently trained to keep their nerve and their discipline. They adopted the more manageable three-rank formation; and charged at a controlled pace, firing one of each man's pair of pistols at a realistic range, before closing sword in hand. Unlike the Royalists, Roundhead troopers were drilled to keep their heads and obey the recall trumpets so that they could make more than one charge, switching direction and target as the battle took shape. Their leaders had also learned - and increasingly had the resources - to hold back reserves to exploit an opportunity or turn back a threat.

Until the end of the war the blazing Cavalier charge might still win the hour - but not the day: typically, by the time they straggled back after chasing their immediate opponents across half a county, the Roundheads had regrouped and were cutting the surrounded Royalist infantry to pieces.

*   *   *

Mounted re-enactment obviously presents difficulties unknown to infantry units of the Sealed Knot and English Civil War Society. Only a small number of the overall membership are experienced riders, and even fewer can provide their own mounts. At a major muster it is normal to see one unit of 12 horse on each side, though for special events larger numbers can be assembled. There were 44 mounted re-enactors at the 1992 Edgehill muster; and the large combined SK/ECWS re-enactment of the battle of Powick Bridge in the same year saw 120 horse take the field.

The established cavalry regiments are Prince Rupert's Lifeguard of Horse and Sir William Waller's Lifeguard of Horse (SK), and Grenville's and Hungerford's Regiments (ECWS); these units recruit nationally. In addition, a number of regiments of foot have their own cavalry or dragoon troops recruited from their own areas. The SK has a maximum of about 100 riders, the ECWS about 50; some transfer from infantry units, others are recruited directly into the cavalry. Each unit has a number of owner-riders, but most horses are hired for musters.

Two stables have particularly specialised in hiring mounts for Civil War re-enactments: Joan Bomford's Mayfield Stables, near Evesham, which has been mounting SK troopers since the 1970s, and Wilf Thomas's Pegasus Riding Centre near Abergavenny. Mayfield Stables can provide, e.g., 24 horses in two specialist vehicles, complete with grooms to care for and saddle the horses. (Muster organisers are expected to prepare a budget, and organise sponsorship, to cover the cost of horse hire and owner-riders' expenses, as well as powder, cannon transport expenses, on-site facilities, etc.; any profits are donated to charity.)

The Sealed Knot's Master of Horse visits the sites, checking suitability, vehicle access, water, grazing, secure areas, owner-rider facilities, etc.; he must bear in mind that horses which are not stablemates may not mix peacefully. The Saturday morning of a muster is used for training, tests, and allocation of mounts. Riders are tested to the level of the British Horse Society Grade 2 examination; and in their ability to obey cavalry commands, which are given in 17th century terminology. A rider experienced in another discipline, e.g. dressage, may not be suitable for service in re-enactment cavalry.

The horses do not have any special training prior to a re-enacted battle unless it is their first time out; in that case they will be ridden among troops with colours and drums, and will have swords brandished around their heads. Animals hired from the regular stables are already well accustomed to the sights and sounds of action, and have a calming effect on newcomers; most horses behave better in the company of others, particularly stablemates. Highly strung horses are avoided, and any animal which is being difficult is removed from the field.

(**Right**) Parliamentary trooper attached to John Bright's Regiment of Foot, ECWS, photographed at Clifford's Tower, York. Apart from the absent "lobster pot" helmet he wears full authentic equipment; the helmet would be replaced when possible by the more comfortable hat. The "harquebusier's" protective equipment included steel back-and-breast plates; a sleeved, long-skirted "buff coat"; and massive bucket-topped boots, which would be pulled up to cover the thigh when riding. The long, single-edged "backsword", slung here from a broad baldric, was a deadly weapon particularly against fleeing infantry - the greatest casualties were always suffered by defeated troops, and when given the chance cavalry turned rout into butchery. This example is of "Walloon" style.

The "buff coat" (like the baldric, this example is a copy of one used by Popham's Horse, which survive in the important Littlecote collection) was originally made from so-called "buffalo" leather, but in practice Civil War coats were of cow or ox hide. This was treated by an oil-tanning process which rendered it flexible and proofed it against decay or hardening - efficiently, to judge by the state of the several surviving examples after 350 years. The process also gave the leather a light yellowish shade; and as they could not be cleaned, coats were subsequently plastered over with an ochre dye to cover wear and tear, enhancing the yellow colour.

Even a poor quality Civil War buff coat was, at £1 10s., costlier than a steel cuirass; and a fine example cost £10 - the same as a good cavalry horse. They could turn sword cuts, and some claim that they could stop a musket ball - though this can only have been at extreme range. At up to about 25lbs. weight a cavalry coat was almost half as heavy as body armour, while allowing easier arm movement in the diagonal plane. This example by Mark Beabey is a superb reproduction of a Littlecote House coat using authentic materials, tanning methods and construction techniques.

(Left) Member of Sir Edward Hungerford's Regiment of Horse, ECWS, at Basing House. He wears the classic "lobster pot" helmet, which is found differing widely in quality and details of design. Single visor bars are associated with Dutch-made imports (probably more likely to be used by Royalist troops), and triple bars with English-made helmets (and thus, Parliamentarian supplies). The steel body armour was often claimed to be proof against pistol balls, but seems to have varied widely in degree of protection - and the thicker the metal, the heavier and more exhausting it was to wear. (A proofing mark, a dent supposedly showing that the maker had tested the plate with a pistol, can be seen at right above the sash in the photo below.)

A reproduction helmet today costs about £65; back-and-breast plates, £65-£80; and a cavalry sword, about £75. Hungerford's do not use firearms, but our subject poses here with a superb long-barrelled wheellock carbine-pistol.

(Right) Detail of the wheellock pistol. Because it was impossible to handle matchlock weapons on horseback, the pairs of pistols normally carried holstered at the saddlebow by Civil War cavalrymen were flintlocks or wheellocks (the latter seem to have figured significantly among Royalist imports from France). The wheellock, set off by a spark struck by a clockwork spring revolving a serrated steel wheel against a piece of iron pyrites, shared the main advantages of the flintlock. It could be wound up in advance (with a "spanner" like a large Allen key), and fired when needed. But it was complex, expensive to buy and maintain, and rather fragile for field conditions, often jamming or breaking.

Pistols came in many designs, usually between 16 and 24ins. long, with bores of between 20 and 36 balls to the pound weight. They were fired held on their side with the priming pan upwards, to ensure a good contact between the priming and the touch-hole. Tests with a large calibre wheellock pistol made in about 1620 have given impressive results - an 85% chance of hitting a man-sized target, and penetration of 2mm of steel plate, at 30 yards (though under perfect range conditions). Most Civil War use seems to have been at point-blank range.

Reproduction wheellocks used by re-enactors can cost around £1,000 a pair. Since neither wheellocks nor the cheaper flintlocks can easily be reloaded in the saddle some re-enactors carry one dummy with a blank-firing device built in, which allows repeated shots.

It is not known how widely carbines were issued to Civil War cavalry; but contemporary purchase accounts do include the m in large numbers, and several survive in collections. Carbines seem to have had a barrel length of 2ft.-2ft.6ins., and were carried from a baldric by a spring clip and ring-and-bracket arrangement. Bores seem to have varied between 24 balls to the pound (i.e. about .4in.) to full musket bore or even slightly larger.

(**Left**) Cavalry officer, Bright's Regiment, ECWS, at Clifford's Tower, York; the red sash was not exclusively a Royalist officer's insignia. The sword worn here from an oil-tanned leather baldric is a swept-hilt rapier: typical of the personal weapons which the gentry would have taken to war in 1642, but rather light for a cavalryman's battle weapon. He also carries an all-purpose dirk in his square-toed, straight-cut, high-top boot. (The legs of this style were made from a single piece of hide; strictly, the term "bucket-top" should only apply to those which had an extra, flared section sewn on above the knee.) Cavalry re-enactors who wish to avoid the cost (£250-300) of made-to-measure reproduction boots sometimes use naval surplus deck boots with added extensions.

The buff coat is of an ornate style appropriate for a well-to-do officer, and was copied by Mark Beabey from that in a famous portrait of Nathaniel Fiennes. Unlike the coat illustrated on page 37, made with four full-length body sections, the Fiennes coat has four torso and four flared skirt sections. Its most noticeable feature is the double construction of the sleeves, the thick, protective outer sleeve with a scalloped cutaway in the elbow to allow easier movement of the arm in the thinner, full-length inner sleeve. There is evidence that some coats were completely "doubled" - i.e. there were two complete bodies, the thick outer one with shorter cut-away sleeves sewn over a thinner coat with full-length sleeves.

(**Right**) Detail of the "Fiennes" buff coat, which weighs over 27lbs. Note the construction, with butt-stitching rather than overlapped seams. Such coats would be made to measure for their owners. Museum examples are usually lined, or partly so, with woollen, linen or silk material. Fastening varies from simple leather laces, to leather buttons, to metal hooks-and-eyes. A fine reproduction of, e.g., the coat on page 37 costs today from £400 unlined, £650 lined; one like this would be nearer £850. Re-enactors who have invested in them report that it can take two years' use to get them fairly pliable, and that the arms can never straighten fully as the sleeves are cut on the curve. Buff coats are also sensitive to temperature, and as stiff as a board in very cold weather; weighing as much as a Vietnam helicopter pilot's ceramic body armour, they are exhausting and overheating to wear for more than a couple of hours at a stretch.

(**Left**) Parliamentarian officer of horse at Basing House: one of Cromwell's "plain russet-coated captains who knew what he fought for and loved what he knew". He wears the Earl of Essex's tawny sash, tied realistically high, over his sword baldric; and note the outer boot-hose. He carries a reproduction mid-17th century flintlock pistol; these have to be made up around reproduction locks since no complete authentic replicas are currently available, and cost £250-300. He also carries a saddle cover of authentic design (which, like the buff coat, this re-enactor made for himself).

(**Left**) Weston Super Mare, SK: at this muster Parliamentary cavalry temporarily changed sides to thicken up Prince Rupert's ranks for a pre-battle cameo. SK Royalist cavalry wear blue doublets and red sashes; not all wear back-and-breast armour, or helmets, and the latter vary – this example is a quite ornate fluted Continental *zischagge* style. Parliamentarian horse wear buff coats, cuirasses, helmets and orange sashes. Many of them also have saddle covers made in Civil War style, as here; these cost about £30. Prince Rupert's mostly use quilted saddle cloths, which look acceptable at a distance. The difficulty of obtaining authentic-looking tack has already been mentioned; but the SK Master of Horse discourages such modern-looking items as nylon girths, numnahs and sheepskin nosebands.

(**Right**) Weston Super Mare, SK: a husband and wife, both riders with the Parliamentarian cavalry, preparing in the horse lines for a pre-battle cameo in which horse of both armies combined. After a demonstration of dragoon tactics they made a massed charge into "dead ground" against an imaginary enemy out of the crowd's line of sight. The fancy green velvet cap may cover a hard hat of some kind, compulsory by SK Board of Safety regulations. Royalists may wear a metal "secrete" under a felt hat, or a riding cap inside a Montero. Up to a third of Sealed Knot cavalry are women, reflecting the greater numbers of horsewomen than men in this country; many are long-serving members, and fight in battle re-enactments with equal determination to their male comrades.

41

(**Above**) At Powick Bridge a combined Sealed Knot and English Civil War Society muster allowed the assembly of 120 mounted cavalry. Here Hungerford's Regiment of the Roundhead Association, ECWS, ride through the English countryside in buff and steel - a splendid sight, and slightly eerie for 1992.

(**Left**) Powick Bridge: the commander of Hungerford's Regiment confers with his trumpeter. At Powick Bridge officers did not wear buff leather, but black coats. Like drummers of foot, Civil War cavalry trumpeters were richly clothed at unit expense, often with open hanging or false sleeves. The trumpet banner often bore some element of the commander's heraldic arms.

(**Below**) Powick Bridge: Sir William Waller's Lifeguard of Horse, SK, at the canter, followed by dragoons on smaller horses. Note the shoulder pauldrons worn by the centre officer; and "WWH" breastplates on the harness, left foreground.

(**Above**) Powick Bridge: an owner-rider in Parliament's ranks, wearing sheepskin under his cuirass both for comfort and to prevent the armour wearing away his buff coat, which has detachable sleeves laced into place.

(**Left**) Weston Super Mare, SK: the commander (right) of Prince Rupert's Lifeguard of Horse with the cornet - junior troop officer - carrying the unit standard. Each troop of Civil War cavalry had a standard; they were about 2ft. square, usually fringed, and bore a wide variety of designs - religious and political motifs and mottoes were popular. They seem generally to have lacked the identification systems found on infantry company colours.

(**Below**) Powick Bridge: the commander of Grenville's Horse, King's Army, ECWS, gives the battle cry; the trumpet sounds; and (**opposite**) the Cavalier charge thunders down on the enemy.

Very few Civil War units wore full "cuirassier" armour - the last echo of the medieval knight - with a "close" helmet or a burgonet and full torso, shoulder, arm and thigh armour. Although it gave very good protection it was expensive, difficult to maintain for whole units on campaign, and exhaustingly heavy and hot to fight in for a generation of men who - unlike their ancestors - had not been raised from boyhood to bear it. After the rout, at Roundway Down in July 1643, of Parliamentarian Sir Arthur Haslerigge's regiment of so-called "Lobsters", cuirassier armour was probably only seen worn by some individual commanders (for its "knightly" prestige) and their bodyguards. However, the torso and arm sections of such armour were practical for use on their own, and were no doubt retained by those who had them, trading a little extra weight for improved protection. It was not unusual for earlier, even Elizabethan helmets and armour to be pressed into service from family armouries.

(Left) Second Battle of Newbury, SK: burgonet, rerebraces and tassets being tried on in Merchant's Row. (Below) Weston Super Mare, SK: a member of Prince Rupert's Lifeguard of Horse wearing a burgonet and pauldrons.

(Above left) Powick Bridge: the commander of Prince Rupert's Lifeguard, SK, in combat with the commander of Hungerford's Horse, Roundhead Association, ECWS. Single combats in front of the crowd are almost always practised and "choreographed" beforehand.

(Left) Powick Bridge: cavalry mêlée between the Cavaliers of Grenville's and the Roundhead troopers of Hungerford's. About 20 riders were unhorsed during this muster, but suffered no serious injuries; no more than slightly dazed and winded, they followed their training and lay still, letting the horses avoid them until the battle swirled away.

Dragoons

Both sides in the Civil War fielded serveral units of dragoons. These were essentially "mounted infantry", enjoying the mobility of horse but dismounting to fight as skirmishing infantry. Various 17th century commentaries lay differing emphasis on their infantry/ cavalry roles, some recommending tactics for firing from the saddle; but in practice they seem mostly to have fought on foot while horse holders guarded their mounts. They were very useful for patrolling, foraging, local security and outpost duties. In pitched battles they were used in support of conventional cavalry, firing from cover on the flanks, or as a "forlorn hope" to seize advanced positions.

(**Left**) Roundway Down, SK: a dismounted dragoon of Wardlaw's Regiment with a political pamphlet tucked in his hat – a Civil War practice among Roundhead activists. Some Civil War dragoon regiments had to serve on foot for months before even receiving horses.

At the Powick Bridge muster, which was organised by the Commandery at Worcester, there was a display of dragoon tactics by a combined unit 92 strong; riding up to their objective, they dismounted to fight on foot while SK cavalry troopers led their horses away.

(**Below**) Pendennis Castle SK muster: dragoons of Slanning's, showing (left) a wheellock carbine, and (right) the single "bridle-gauntlet" often worn by mounted men to protect their rein-hand and forearm - slashing at an opponent's reins or left hand to rob him of control over his horse was a common ploy in cavalry mêlées.

(**Above left**) Powick Bridge: a dragoon of Slanning's Regiment, SK, "a sturdy Welsh cob with a sturdy rider". Note the slung musket: some New Model Army dragoons were provided with flintlocks, but given their infantry tactics at least some units certainly carried matchlocks; and some kind of sling would have been necessary. Dragoon horses, and saddles, are recorded as costing only about half as much as their cavalry equivalents.

(**Left**) Weston Super Mare, SK: Slanning's Dragoons advance on foot. Note the swallow-tailed dragoon guidon; and (left foreground) an officer with a pair of rapiers - an archaic fashion for gentlemen. There is no real evidence for dragoon dress and equipment; a treatise of 1639 recommends buff coats and open-face helmets, but infantry dress, perhaps with boots, was probably the norm during the Civil War, with a Montero or some other cap.

Guns

Civil War artillery came in as motley an array of sizes and designs as all other equipment. Cannon ranged from the little "robinet" weighing 120lbs., firing a ¾lb. ball of 1¼in. calibre, to the 4 ton, 8in. calibre "cannon royal" firing a 63lb. ball with a 40lb. powder charge. Artillery was of central importance in the many sieges around which the regional campaigns of the field armies often revolved. Trains of artillery were dragged laboriously around the country by large horse teams over bad dirt roads, which they ploughed into dusty, brick-hard ruts in dry weather and impassable quagmires in the rain; and ultimately decided the outcome of sieges by battering down city walls and castle towers. Large calibre, short range mortars dropped explosive shells into towns with devastating effect, often starting serious fires.

In pitched battles cannon were less effective, being generally too unwieldy for movement around the battlefield. Artillery was very frightening; was widely hated as a devilish, inhuman weapon; and could cause hideous local casualties amongst formed-up infantry; but it seldom seriously affected, and never decided, the outcome of battles of manoeuvre.

At Naseby, June 1645, the King fielded 12 guns: two "demi cannon" weighing 6,000lbs., firing 27lb. shot of 6in. calibre, and needing a nine-man crew; two "demi-culverin" (3,600lbs., 4½in. calibre, 9lbs., six crew); and eight "sakers" (about 2,500lbs., 3½in. calibre, 5-6lb. shot, six crew). A saker's flat-trajectory range was around 300 yards, its maximum carrying range about 1,500 yards.

Guns were slow to load: five to six minutes for the middle-range sakers and demi-cannon. The muzzle-loaded barrel had to be carefully scoured and swabbed of debris or sparks from the last shot, and the touch-hole

(Above) Second Newbury, SK: 4in. guns manned by Edward Montague, Earl of Manchester's Regiment fire in battery. Some re-enactment units are purely artillery; others are companies within foot regiments, with one or more guns. SK gunners, like their Civil War originals, tend to be independent spirits and something of a law unto themselves.

cleaned. Powder was then ladled down the bore from an open "budge barrel" brought up to the muzzle, and tamped with a wad of straw or dry grass; the ball was rolled in, and secured with a second wad. The touch-hole was filled with fine priming powder from the gunner's flask; and the gun was fired with smouldering slowmatch held in a linstock. Throughout Civil War armies the accidental meeting of exposed powder with sparks or naked flame was commonplace, and lethal; when it involved the large stocks found in artillery lines or ammunition wagons it could be disastrous enough to affect the course of a battle.

In an age when the mathematical skills needed for gunnery were extremely rare, experienced gunners were respected as the masters of a scientific mystery. In high demand, they were highly paid; often Dutch or German mercenaries, they would be offered incentives to change sides if captured.

The greatest number of reproduction guns used at any re-enactment muster was 26, at Second Newbury in 1989. Several times this number of guns are owned by various units, but many are incomplete or unserviceable at any given time. Most are of small size, for economic and practical reasons, and are classed as robinets. All guns must comply with legal proofing requirements, and are tested by the Birmingham Proof House; some are proofed for shot, others for powder and wad only.

(**Left**) A 3in. gun of an SK Parliamentary unit ready to move, with its tools and powder box in position. The sliding escutcheon plate covering the touch-hole is not authentic, but a safety feature. Most guns tend not to be exact replicas of 17th century designs, but give a reasonable impression from a distance. Guns are made by group members, taking wooden patterns from 18th or 19th century barrels and casting in iron or brass (the latter easier to cast, but more expensive). The cost of casting a 4in. barrel 8-9ft. long was about £1,100 in 1991. The King's Lifeguard have a gun made from high tensile steel tube covered in fibreglass, which is fully proofed but very light. There is a school of thought in the SK that larger bores should be reduced by sleeving, for economy of powder and (supposedly) increased safety; but this is far from a generally held view.

(**Right**) Pendennis Castle, SK: gunners of Sir Bevil Grenvile's Regiment, distinguished by hooped black sleeves, with their No.2 gun, a brass fawconet named "Caesar's Due". It was made by Harry Stocker (third left), Battery Commander of the Parliamentary Army, SK, and Powder Master West of England.

(Right) Edgehill, SK: a very small robinet on an A-frame carriage. At left, note the head of the linstock used for firing cannon: it holds a length of match lit at both ends, and sometimes has a blade which could be used in hand-to-hand fighting.

At re-enactments the classic arrangement for a gun position is a triangle, with the linstock stuck in the ground down-wind, and the powder box holding measured, bagged charges up-wind of the gun. For legal reasons the gun captain in each crew, who is responsible at all times for the powder, must hold a Black Powder Certificate; and one crew member, a Shotgun Certificate (if the bore is less than 2in.) or Firearm Certificate (if it is larger).

(Left) Roundway Down, SK: robinet of Sir Marmaduke Rawdon's Regiment. One of the crew protects the touch-hole with her hand, so the piece is presumably loaded. Women are often seen in today's gun crews, despite the fairly heavy physical work involved with the larger pieces, and Ballard's Regiment has an all-female crew.

(Right) Helmsley Castle, Yorks, ECWS: the two most authentic reproduction guns seen at today's re-enactments. Foreground is "Barak", owned by the Roundhead Association, a "bastard culverin" made by Ken Fisher, with a bore of about 3 3/4 ins. and a barrel about three feet shorter than a comparable Civil War piece. In the background is "Raven", a reproduction saker owned by the Royal Armouries, HM Tower of London, made by Austin Colin Carpenter using an original barrel of the 1630s as a model. It was cast by Iron Bros. of Tavistock, with a steel sleeve reducing the bore to 3 inches. The carriage is based on plans dating from the Marlburian period and Civil War specifications. *(Photo by Magic Lantern, courtesy English Heritage Special Events Unit)*

(Left) Pendennis Castle, SK: Royalist fawconet of Sir Nicholas Slanning's Regiment. There are usually about six crew for a medium-size gun. Like Civil War ordnance, reproduction guns are often individually named - "Phoenix", "Sweet Lips", "Magog", etc.; this piece is "Charity". Note the tools at right: a mop and a screw-headed "searcher" or scourer. The bucket holds water for damping the swabbing mop; the hessian sack, wadding material - paper, straw, hay, or grass (cut, not pulled up, to prevent pebbles being rammed in with the wad). At one time small rolls of carpet felt were also used; the tape holding them was supposed to be cut at the last moment so that the roll opened out on firing and did not form a projectile, but forgetfulness over this safety measure led to the use of felt being stopped.

(**Left**) Weston Super Mare, SK: the priming ignites in the touch-hole of a robinet of Sir Thomas Ballard's Regiment.

Powder is purchased centrally by re-enactment societies (at about £3.50 a pound) and sold on to the Muster Master for a particular event; over a whole season the Sealed Knot might use about 3 1/2 tons. It is issued to the legally licensed gun captains, who make up charges of sizes to suit their gun – anything from 1/2oz. for a robinet to 4lbs. for a saker - in plastic bags. These are kept in the powder box, and passed to the gunner at need by the "powder monkey". The gunner puts the bag in the muzzle, then a wad, which is rammed home - the bag itself is never rammed, to prevent it splitting. A pricker is thrust down the touch-hole to pierce the bag; the touch-hole must then be covered by a gloved hand until primed, from a separate flask, and fired with match in a linstock.

(**Right**) Gosport, ECWS: battery of robinets coming under attack at point of pike. The placing of guns at a muster is at the choice of the commander of the Tercio (brigade). Artillery will fight mixed among other troops - as here - when they are permitted, but are most often placed on the flanks. Historically, it would be more authentic for them to fight more closely with their units under the protection of regimental infantry.

Safety regulations state that troops must not approach a loaded gun; a gun captain can order pikemen away, and in keeping troops clear of loaded ordnance he may overrule any other commander - the ultimate responsibility for safety is his alone.

In the centre background, note the small, colourful guidon: this is a commanding officer's personal heraldic flag.

The Camp Ground

M ost re-enactors live on a campsite for the duration of a muster. The organisers provide a suitable area out of sight of the battleground, with latrine, drinking water and washing facilities. Here tents of all colours and sizes blossom among the parked camper vans and caravans. Depending on local regulations camp fires may be lit for outdoor cooking; if not, those who cannot be bothered to brew up on camping stoves will inevitably follow the smell of hot grease to the mobile kitchens of the registered caterers who haunt the re-enactment trail.

As evening falls the troops converge on the light and noise of the one utterly reliable landmark: the beer tent, which forms the social focus of the muster. With access to the campsite restricted to members and their families, re-enactors can relax in the beer tent, often listening to a live band or folk group, and swapping pints and lies with friends and rivals old and new.

Here 20-year veterans can be heard declaring that in the early days costumed members caught in headlights while walking the nightime lanes in search of pubs were often reported as ghosts...And Les retells the one about the Italian tourist in Scotland who came across a uniformed crew dragging a cannon, and told the local police he had spotted bandits in the hills,...And Dave recalls putting his armour on under his coat to avoid

(**Above**) Siege of Carew Castle, SK: an idyllic setting for an authentic historical camp, where a "camp follower" prepares plausible 17th century food using period-style utensils and methods.

paying excess baggage at an airport check-in, and the Customs officer's face when he found what had set off the metal detector...

Quite separate from this site is sometimes found an authentic historical camp set up by the host unit or some other group. The public are allowed into this area, which is usually near the field of battle and which forms part of the actual re-enactment. All modern features are banished from the authentic camp, where the keener "living history" re-enactors may live throughout the muster, showing visitors round and explaining the realities of 17th century life.

(Left) Weston Super Mare, SK: the wife and children of a soldier of the King's Lifeguard of Foot act out their roles in the authentic camp.

In fact, Civil War camps on the march had tents for officers only; letters and memoirs often speak of the misery of sleeping in the open, even though most campaigns were conducted between April and October. During winter armies went into permanent quarters in towns, usually living quite comfortably and being well fed. During the campaign season passing troops were billeted where possible on local householders, who also had to provide food. Sometimes the army issued promissory notes, though they frequently went unpaid; sometimes civilians were simply ordered to provide "free quarter". This was a ruinous system even when not abused, as it often was; the fear of pillage by passing armies of both sides far outweighed political loyalties for most civilians.

(Right) Roundway Down, SK: a pikeman of Earl Rivers' Regiment busies himself with domestic chores, and his little son, during quiet hours in camp. Often whole families will attend a muster, treating it like any other camping holiday. Re-enactment groups encourage family memberships with concessionary subscription rates. Children may join, but are not usually allowed on the battlefield if under 16 years of age.

(Far right) Weston Super Mare, SK: a "camp follower" in the authentic camp. Women may join any fighting unit as full members, but some prefer the camp followers' role; the care they bring to their historical costumes is noticeable. They perform more or less the same roles as their 17th century originals: they care for their men and children in camp; and during battle re-enactments carry water to the combatants, and later search for their menfolk among the slain.

(Right) A soldier of Samuel Jones's Parliamentarian regiment in the authentic campsite at the SK siege of Carew Castle. Re-enactors of any historical period will know how gratefully these troops and their families must welcome this sunny day in a good site: for those caught by heavy rain on a badly drained site the horrors of campaigning can become all too convincing.

Sieges were in fact the most deadly episodes for Civil War troops and civilians. Large camps, static for months, were lethal breeding-grounds of typhoid and bubonic plague - far greater killers than blade or ball; and even in open field campaigning losses from a combination of fatigue, exposure, scanty rations and disease could be enormous.

(Right) Second Newbury, SK:
Bailiff's Forge selling armour on
Traders' Row. Most of a Civil
War re-enactor's needs can be
satisfied from the traders' booths
at musters. Basic clothing may be
home-made, but leather and
metal items have to be obtained
(individually, or by unit bulk
purchase) from specialist
craftsmen. At the larger musters
one may find 30 or 40 traders set
up near the campsite, selling
clothing, shoes, armour, weapons
and leatherwork. The traders are
licensed annually and regulated
by the host re-enactment society.

(**Left**) Pendennis Castle, SK: a young boy takes advantage of one of the simple wooden carts often seen around authentic campsites to practice the campaigner's first lesson: sleep whenever and wherever you get the chance.

(**Right**) The last hours of peace: a pikeman enjoys the beauty of a summer's morning in the rolling landscape of southern England. Roundway Down, SK.

(**Right**) Weston Super Mare, SK: in the authentic camp the Colonel of Bard's Regiment catches a moment of peace by the fire. Despite his burdensome responsibilities, his rank presumably brings immunity from cleaning black iron cauldrons - an unforgettable chore in any re-enactment camp.

The Day
of Battle

(**Above**) A dragoon passes the news of the day with a gun crew of the Parliament's army. Second Newbury, SK.

(**Left**) A quiet scene in an idyllic spot - until you start wondering about that rope... A hanging party prepare to give a spy his quietus. Roundway Down, SK.

(Left) A captain of foot of the Earl of Stamford's Regiment enjoys a last peaceful pipe as the camp stirs around him. Roundway Down, SK.

(Right) Cavalry patrols ghost along the hedgerows, feeling out the shape of the enemy's deployment. Edgehill: Waller's Lifeguard, SK.

(Above left) His Majesty King Charles I approaches the field of Edgehill. He is portrayed here by actor and drama teacher Arthur Starkey.

(Above) Regimental colonels confer with their officers and staff: here, the commanding officer of Carr's Regiment, SK, at Roundway Down.

(Left) The general of the Parliamentarian army emerges from his tent to survey his forces' preparations for battle. Weston Super Mare, SK.

(Above) The moments tick away for an ensign of Parliamentary foot, clutching the colour which he must soon guard with his life. York, ECWS.

(Above right) The Muster Master General discusses a point of deployment with a senior officer of Skippon's. Weston Super Mare, SK.

(Right) "The watchword is *God and the Cause*..." The commander of the Royalist Army of the West, SK, at Pendennis Castle.

(**Above left**) Meanwhile, the humbler soldiers have nothing to do but wait, in what calm they can command: infantry of the sergeant-major's company, James Carr's Regiment, Western Association, SK, at Roundway Down.

(**Above**) For many in the ranks of Parliament's armies their non-conformist faith was a shield against doubt and fear: this pikeman of Carr's, like some of his Civil War forebears, has scribed biblical quotations on his helmet. Roundway Down, SK.

(**Left**) Both sides brought passionate religious conviction to the Civil War, and encouraged chaplains to give rousing sermons before battle. This was particularly marked among the Roundheads, whose chaplains sometimes charged into battle with their units, bible in one hand and weapon in the other; hymns and psalms were often sung by whole regiments as they advanced. At Leeds in June 1644, for instance, one Rev. Jonathan Scholefield led a desperate assault in person, singing the 68th Psalm: "Let God arise, let his enemies be scattered..." Here a soberly dressed chaplain exhorts Colonel James Wardlaw's Dragoons to fight for God and Parliament: Roundway Down, SK.

(**Above**) Infantry form up for battle at Roundway Down; the Lord General of the Royalist army reviews the Prince Palatine's Tercio, consisting of Prince Rupert's and Earl Rivers' Regiments of Foot, SK. When only small units are represented at a muster they are brigaded together; in case of equal ranks, the officer with the largest number of men takes command. There is an officers' briefing at Tercio level, which is then relayed to the junior ranks. Most re-enacted battles follow the historical events, and with the same outcome, although it is not always possible to refight them on the actual historical sites. On the rare occasions when a battle which is not historically documented is re-enacted, a result is determined by carefully following 17th century tactics.

A Civil War field army's infantry were usually drawn up for a pitched battle in at least two lines of units, the regiments placed chequerboard-fashion so that the intervals in the front line were covered by units in the second line. Artillery pieces were also placed in some of the gaps between units. The horse were drawn up on each wing in at least two lines of units, similarly arranged. A reserve of cavalry might be held back behind the centre or one flank. On the extreme flanks, either extending the frontage, advanced under cover, or "refused", there might be units of dragoons or detached musketeers; and a small force might be pushed forward in some exposed position - or to seize one - as a so-called "forlorn hope".

(**Right**) A dismounted dragoon readies his musket as the troops move towards their positions. Roundway Down, SK.

65

(Previous pages, 66-67)
The Royalist army, SK, forms for battle at Edgehill. In the foreground, troopers of Prince Rupert's Lifeguard of Horse; right, the Royal Standard, and beyond it the pikes of Sir Nicholas Slanning's Regiment; in the distance, the King's Lifeguard of Foot march on.

During the Civil War major battles might involve armies of between 10,000 and 15,000 men on each side. The largest was Marston Moor, in July 1644, fought by a total of around 46,000 men. (About 1,500 Parliamentarians and between 3,000 and 4,000 Royalists died there, and we may assume that the wounded totalled slightly more than the dead.)

Soldiers usually came to the field after a punishing march, and several comfortless nights in the open. Long, straggling columns of men, horses, guns and wagons ruined the dirt roads, and there were few reliable maps; a unit might average only eight or ten miles a day for many hours of toil. In May-July 1644, for instance, William Waller's infantry marched on 36 out of 69 days; spent no more than three nights in one place; and slept in the open, during a very wet summer, for 21 of those nights. Although the official scale of

rations - bread, meat, cheese, beans or peas, and beer - was fairly generous, its issue when on the march was unpredictable. When an army finally stood for battle the men were often tired, hungry and thirsty as they waited in their ranks for hours on end, thinking about the ordeal to come.

The Civil War did not, in fact, involve many large-scale pitched battles between major field armies; of the total combat casualties it has been calculated that only about 15% were suffered in major actions involving 1,000 or more dead. It was mainly a war of fairly small, dispersed forces manoeuvring and fighting for regional supremacy. Most of the soldiers of the Civil War spent much of their time in garrisons of a few hundred foot and horse controlling an area of the countryside, and living off it - sometimes in a cruelly oppressive way. Numerically, more than half of the 650-odd recorded engagements involved less than 250 dead. Most of these were encounters between small forces - patrols, small units attacking neighbouring garrisons or "beating up" enemy billets, or the merciless plundering expeditions which made life a misery for civilians.

(Above left) A trumpeter of horse leads Royalist musketeers from Owen's and other regiments into their place in the battle line. Edgehill, SK.

(Left) On the Parliamentarian flank a troop of horse stamp and fidget as they await the order to advance, their commander at their head with his cornet standard-bearer and trumpeter. Hungerford's Horse at Powick Bridge, SK/ECWS.

(Above) At last, the tension breaks: Hungeford's troopers advance into battle. Powick Bridge, SK/ECWS.

(Left) The first clash of infantry: a captain of the Earl of Stamford's Regiment leads his pikemen in the defence of a hastily fortified position. Roundway Down, SK.

(Right) Parliamentarian pike struggle to hold their position against a determined attack by Royalist foot and horse. Western Association, SK, Roundway Down.

Royalist musketeers of
Blackwell's Regiment of Foot,
Duke of York's Brigade, advance
among the fallen in their
authentic six-deep files, with
their drummer, sergeant and
officer on the flank. Gosport,
ECWS.

(Above left & above)
The most feared weapon in the King's armoury: Prince Rupert's Lifeguard of Horse unleash a charge. Edgehill, SK.

The outcome of cavalry charges (in any period of military history) was decided more by nerve than by the actual physical shock. No horse, unless maddened by pain or panic, will charge full tilt into a solid mass of armed men and other horses - at the last moment it will always swerve or pull up. Rupert's cavalry owed their mastery of so many fields to their boldness and high morale. The heart-stopping sight of a wave of armed riders bearing down, knee to knee and yelling like fiends above the thunder of thousands of hooves, is enough to make all but the steadiest troops break and run. Once the opposing infantry or cavalry lost their formation they became a mob of individual victims, and the Cavaliers hunted them mercilessly, leaving their butchered bodies strewn across miles of countryside. If a solidly formed body of pike or shot held their ground and waited until the cavalry came within range they were more or less invulnerable to all but a thin hail of pistol balls.

(Below left) Prince Rupert's Lifeguard attack infantry of Hammond's Regiment and the London Trained Bands. In today's re-enactment battles musketeers do not generally fire when horses are closer than 35 yards in any direction.

(Overleaf, pages 74-75) The ultimate test for Civil War infantry: advancing to contact at point of pike. With pikes in the "charge" position a unit's front rank each had the pikeheads of the two or three men behind them in file thrusting forward past their shoulders. Pushed by the ranks behind, who waited to press forward into the place of those who fell, they advanced onto the enemy's pikeheads.... "Push of pike" must have called for great strength, and cold-blooded courage the front rank men - could hardly move to protect themselves in the press. In most battles this exhausting, bloody scrum probably lasted only a few moments before one side began to waver. It would have been the rear ranks which gave way first - they could tell what was awaiting them at the front as the ranks wore away, and, unlike the front ranks, they could still move freely enough to try to escape. The spark of panic would spread through the close-packed mass in a moment, and once a unit's formation began to break up it was lost. Once one unit in the battle - line broke, the enemy could press forward through the gap to take other units in the flanks and rear, "rolling up" the whole line. Devereux's Regiment, Roundhead Association, ECWS, at Gosport.

(**Above & above right**) The Parliamentarian infantry of Fairfax's Brigade (Overton's, Walton's, Foxe's and Devereux's Regiments) face pike of the King's Army: Gosport, ECWS. In re-enactments pikemen fight "at point" only to gain ground, though some claim that it is actually safer than the alternative method with pikes slanted. Although all battles are "scripted", if a regiment do not give ground they have it taken from them. Every unit aims to win the confrontations even if history dictates that they lose the battle. Some regiments are known to fight hard, and expect resistance. Close fighting gives a surge of adrenalin, which has to be controlled to avoid injuries.

(**Below left**) A sergeant of pike in Sir Gilbert Hoghton's Company, wearing a burgonet helmet and a "Dutch coat" over his armour: Weston Super Mare, SK. Sergeants in re-enactment units work their way up through the ranks, and are chosen by their regimental officers. Their duties are to keep rank and file, enforce discipline, and pass on officers' orders.

(**Right**) Royalist's eye view of Roundhead Association pikemen of Fairfax's Brigade: Gosport, ECWS.

77

(**Left**) Pendennis Castle, SK: Royalist gun crew scouring their piece after firing, to scrape out any debris before they reload. This is followed by swabbing with a wet mop to extinguish any final spark, and then with a dry mop, although plastic bags protect the powder charges from damp.

The artillery have many long-serving members who collaborate to ensure maximum safety through strict training, controls and supervision. One veteran told the authors that he could only recall four accidents in 22 years. The authors happened to witness one of these, when a gun went off while being rammed. The ramrod was blown for some distance, and the gunner received burns (from which he made a complete recovery after hospital treatment).

(**Below**) Robinet of Sir Thomas Ballard's Regiment firing - the camera lens foreshortens the distance between gun and infantry rather over-dramatically. Weston Super Mare, SK.

(**Right**) Officer and pikemen of Fairfax's Brigade at close quarters: Gosport,ECWS. The man at left has a green tape tied round his arm, the Civil War sign of the Levellers, an extremist Roundhead movement.

(**Above**) Parliamentarian cavalry
charging past Royalist infantry:
the commander of Waller's Horse
with, background, pikemen of Sir
Nicholas Slanning's, Sir Gilbert
Hoghton's and the Marquis of
Newcastle's Foot. Weston Super
Mare, SK.

(**Left**) Troopers get in amongst
fleeing infantry as a barricaded
strongpoint falls. Roundway
Down, SK.

(**Above**) If infantry held their ground, forming a "stand" of pike, the cavalry could do little to break them. Note the fluted, antique-style lance for the troop standard - an authentic touch. Waller's Horse at Edgehill, SK.

(**Right**) A veteran of Waller's Horse adjusts his bridle-gauntlet. By 1648 a majority of troopers in the elite Roundhead cavalry regiments had served together for six years; the quality of these units is understandable. Second Newbury, SK.

(Above, left, & above right)
Under a dramatic sky full of
racing clouds, Royalist
musketeers supported by Prince
Rupert's Lifeguard of Horse
engage Parliamentarian pike of
Ballard's, Carr's, and the Tower
Hamlets Trained Bands. Weston
Super Mare, SK.

(Right) A final volley of shot
from Sir Marmaduke Rawdon's
Royalist musketeers as the
infantry lines come together.
Weston Super Mare, SK.

(**Top left & right**) The last shots
fired, musketeers reverse their
weapons and rush forward to
fight hand-to-hand with the butts.
This was a recognised tactic, not
an act of individual desperation
(the 17th century command was
"Fall on pell-mell!"); the heavy
musket with its angular butt was
a murderous skull-crusher.
Edgehill, SK.

(**Left**) A last desperate pike
charge as the climax of battle
approaches. Second Newbury,
SK.

(**Left**) A trooper of Prince Rupert's Lifeguard comes to hand-to-hand with a doubly-armed Highlander: Rannoch's Company of Sword, SK, at Weston Super Mare.

(**Right**) Parliamentarian officer and Royalist pikeman struggling over a barricade: Second Newbury, SK.

(**Left**) Re-enactment is a "contact sport", and battles can become heated between units which enjoy particular rivalry. Pendennis Castle, SK.

(**Below**) A Royalist officer "kills" a disarmed enemy musketeer. Summary execution of prisoners, almost unknown in the early campaigns, became more common as the bitter years of civil war dragged on. Edgehill, SK.

Now the hurly-burly's done,
now the battle's lost and won...
It should perhaps be remembered
(if only briefly, and without false
solemnity) that the events which
these historical re-enactment
societies recreate today in
comradeship and good humour,
for their own interest in history
and the crowds' enjoyment of
colourful spectacle, were among
the most devastating in British
history.

It has been calculated that in
England and Wales alone battle
deaths between 1642 and 1651
may have totalled 85,000, to which
must be added about 100,000
military and civilian deaths from
war-related disease. From a total
population of perhaps five million,
that loss represents 3.7% - which
should be compared with 2.6% of
the population of the British Isles
dead in the First, and 0.6% in the
Second World Wars. In Scotland

and Ireland local hatreds brought a
particular savagery to the Civil War
campaigns, and losses were
proportionately much higher.

In the early campaigns in
England "Cavaliers" and
"Roundheads" might call each
other "Papist dogs" and "rebel
rogues", but there is much evidence
that they respected each other's
courage and sincerity, however
misguided. This tolerance largely
disappeared during the Second and

Third Civil Wars, which were
fought with ruthless determination.

The harsh lessons learnt during
the war, and the decade of military
rule which followed, have shaped
British political history. It may be
argued that the relative civil peace
and order which we have enjoyed
since those years is our legacy from
those who risked everything, and
often gave it, for King or
Parliament on the battlefields of the
1640s.

The Sweets of Victory

Some members of re-enactment
societies take their interest in the
arts, crafts and daily life of 17th
century England beyond the purely
military aspects. Some go to great
trouble and expense to equip
themselves for demanding "living
history" recreations of civil as well
as military life. Apart from the
displays which they put on for the
public and for educational bodies,
these enthusiasts meet privately to
enjoy each others' company and to
share their knowledge.

Most of these pictures were taken
at a costumed banquet held by
members of the Sealed Knot in a
17th century hall at Abingdon.

(Previous page) A cavalry trooper
in Sir William Waller's Lifeguard
of Horse, relaxing off duty in
civilian finery: she is Francine
Pimperton, in the blue.

(Above) Foreground, Sue and
Mark Hargreaves, who make and
sell lace and glassware for
re-enactors.

(Right) A pensive and sombrely
dressed diner. His fine lace collar,
and the discreet richness of his
clothing, show that he is not a true
Puritan.

(Opposite) A fine, painterly study
of Mark Hargreaves.

(**Above**) Geoff and Caroline Vincent, members of Earl Rivers' Regiment of Foot. Like many female members of these groups Caroline makes all her own costumes; it is extremely time-consuming and demanding, involving in-depth research and many hours of painstaking needlework.

(**Left**) The hairstyle is copied carefully from period portraits, the gown from a surviving example; the beauty spot would have been painted on in the 17th century.

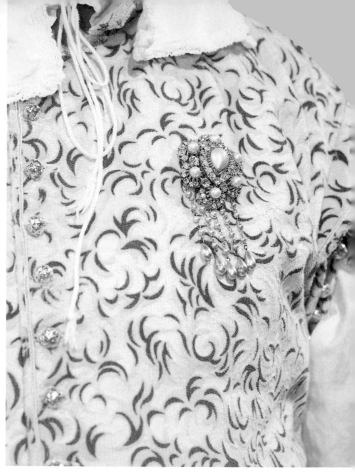

(**Above left & right**) Details of fine quality reconstructed 1640s female (left) and male costume - women did not have a monopoly of rich embroidery. Such workmanship would have been very expensive in the 17th century, involving costly silks and bullion wire. Today, with less expensive materials, the main investment for those with the necessary skill is time. Although most members make their own "dress" costumes there are a few specialists - such as the Civil Wardrobe - making such clothing for sale.

(**Right**) An aptly posed study of pewterer Clive Simpson at table.

(**Right**) John Cartwright, the regimental chaplain to Earl Rivers' Regiment, is a vicar in real life. Here he officiates at the christening of a child of a member of the regiment; the entire regiment attended, all - including the infant - in authentic 17th century costume.

(**Left**) Will Hughes, a Royalist officer of Sir John Owen's Regiment, Welsh Militia, pays court to a lady-in-waiting.

Basic Chronology of the English Civil War

1642

After years of dispute over constitutional and religious prerogatives between King and Parliament, King Charles I leaves London for York *(May)*. Final negotiations fail; King calls upon loyal subjects for aid in crushing rebellion, and formally raises his standard *(22 August)*.

23 Sept.: Royalist general Prince Rupert defeats Nathaniel Fiennes at Powick Bridge. King gains narrow advantage over Parliamentarian Earl of Essex in confused battle at Edgehill *(23 Oct.)*; occupies Oxford as his headquarters; marches on London.

13 Nov.: Rupert turns back from London when blocked by Essex with London Trained Bands at Turnham Green.

1643

Sporadic regional warfare throughout year, each side enjoying mixed fortunes as many towns are taken and retaken. In the south and west main Royalist general is Sir Ralph Hopton; Parliamentary champion is Sir William Waller. In the north and Midlands Sir Thomas Fairfax and his father, for Parliament, mainly fight the Earl of Newcastle. Periodically the main Royalist "Oxford" army, under the King and Rupert, and the Earl of Essex's Roundhead army, manoeuvre against each other or the enemy's regional armies.

19 Jan.: Hopton victorious at Braddock Down. Prince Maurice defeats Waller near Tewkesbury *(13 April)*. Part of Essex's army beaten by Rupert at Chalgrove Field *(18 June)*. Newcastle defeats Fairfax near Bradford. Hopton and Waller fight costly, indecisive battle at Lansdown Hill *(5 July)*. The Queen brings the King important munitions from the Continent. Waller routed by Wilmot and Byron at Roundway Down *(13 July)*. Rupert captures Bristol *(26 July)*. Oliver Cromwell founds his reputation by cavalry victory near Gainsborough. Roundhead defeat at Torrington; Exeter surrendered to Royalists *(4 Sept.)*. Essex defeats King at First Newbury *(20 Sept.)*. Parliament ratifies Solemn League and Covenant with Scots *(25 Sept.)*; King negotiates for troops from Ireland. Cromwell and Fairfax beat Royalists at Winceby *(11 October)*.

1644

Jan.: Fairfax successful in north; Earl of Leven leads Scots army south to aid Parliament. Waller defeats Hopton at Cheriton *(28 March)*. Earl of Newcastle besieged in York by Fairfax and Leven, later joined *(May)* by Earl of Manchester. Waller defeated by King at Cropredy Bridge *(29 June)*. Rupert raises siege of York and is joined by Newcastle.Their 17,000-strong army is defeated by up to 28,000 Roundheads and Scots under Fairfax, Leven and Manchester at Marston Moor *(2 July)*. Royalist Scottish general Montrose beats Lord Elcho at Tippermuir *(1 Sept.)*;

sacks Perth, Aberdeen. The King forces Essex's army to surrender at Lostwithiel *(2 Sept.)*. Waller and Manchester beaten by King at Second Newbury *(27 October)*.

1645

April: Formation, from commands of Essex, Waller and Manchester, of Parliament's New Model Army - permanent, unified force 22,000 strong for nationwide operations, under Sir Thomas Fairfax, Sir Philip Skippon (foot) and Oliver Cromwell (horse). Montrose's Highland and Irish army defeat Covenanters at Auldearn *(9 May)*. The King, with 8,000 men, is decisively defeated by 13,000-strong New Model under Fairfax at Naseby *(14 June)*. Fairfax defeats western Royalists under Goring at Langport *(10 July)*. Montrose inflicts heavy loss on Covenanters at Kilsyth *(15 Aug.)*. Royalist garrisons fall, including Bristol *(10 Sept.)*. Montrose routed by David Leslie at Philiphaugh *(13 September)*.

1646

King Charles surrenders to Scots at Newark *(5 March)*; isolated Royalist garrisons hold out, but the "First Civil War" is over. The King is held by Parliament during prolonged, three-sided negotiations between King, Parliament, and its disaffected army.

1647

King negotiates secretly with Scots while Parliament and army factions wrangle over constitutional settlement.

1648

April: "Second Civil War" - Royalist risings in Wales and south-east, Scottish invasion. Fairfax successful in Kent and Essex *(June)*, and Cromwell in Wales before defeating Royalists at Preston *(17 Aug.)* and Scots at Winwich Pass.

1649

After army republican faction forces trial of King for treason by House of Commons he is beheaded *(30 Jan.)*. Cromwell, chairman of Council of State, ruthlessly crushes Royalist rising in Ireland *(from August)*.

1650

Scots proclaim King Charles II *(May)*: "Third Civil War". Cromwell returns; replaces Fairfax as captain-general; destroys Scots army under Leslie at Dunbar *(3 September)*.

1651

Charles II invades with Scottish army, destroyed by Cromwell at Worcester *(3 Sept.)*; Charles flees abroad. *(1653-58 : Cromwell rules Commonwealth as Lord Protector heading military government.)*

Contact addresses:
Readers who wish to know more about the re-enactment societies featured in this book may contact them through the following addresses:

Sealed Knot Society
Administrative & general enquiries:
Nicholas Bacon
1 Rock Street
Croscombe, Wells
Somerset BA5 3QT
Membership enquiries:
Mrs.Margaret Smith
11 Ings Way
~~...~~ ...one
Sh~~...~~ S30 6GL

English ... ar Society
All enquiries:
The English Civil War Society
70 Hailgate
Howden, nr.Goole
North Humberside DN14 7ST

Authors' note:
All photographs published in this book, except one specifically credited otherwise, are copyright the authors. These, and many other photographs of similar subjects, are held by Collections Picture Library, tel. 081-883 0083.